Fruity Pasta Sensations

By Jane Amparis

© 2014 Jane Amparis

ISBN: Softcover   978-0-6480974-0-2
        eBook   978-0-6480974-1-9

All rights reserved. No part of this book may be reproduced or transmitted in any form or by any means, electronic or mechanical, including photocopying, recording, or by any information storage and retrieval system, without permission in writing from the copyright owner.

Rev. date: 31-May-2017

This book is dedicated to my boys, Riley and James.

You are the apples of my eye. May you have the courage to achieve your dreams.

About The Author

Jane was born and raised in Melbourne, Australia. She grew up in a very strong Italian culture and always enjoyed sharing a meal with the extended family at Nonna's house. Through Nonna's cooking spawned Jane's own deep-seated passion for cooking. It was to be her legacy.

Jane studied at LaTrobe University and completed her Bachelor of Speech Pathology degree. She had married and had been blessed with two beautiful boys. She now has the privilege of raising them full-time. It was during her time staying at home and caring for her babies that 'Fruity Pasta Sensations' was created.

Contents

CREAMY AVOCADO CHICKEN FUSILLI	1
CARAMELISED APPLE WITH RADIATORI IN TOMATO SAUCE	4
HAWAIIAN PASTA BAKE	9
VERMICELLI WITH BREADCRUMBS, TUNA, PARSLEY AND LEMON	11
CREAMY MANGO CHICKEN RIGATONI	15
SPAGHETTI IN SEMI-DRIED TOMATO BUTTER SAUCE	19
ORANGE, CRANBERRY, WALNUT & TURKEY FARFALLE	21
ROAST PUMPKIN, PANCETTA & SWEET ONIONS GNOCCHI	23
DUCK L'ORANGE CURLY TAGLIATELLE	24
RED GRAPE & CHICKEN ROLLINI	29
LIME LAMB WITH SPINACH FETTUCCINE	31
BLUEBERRY RICOTTA CANNELLONI	33
CHOCOLATE RASPBERRY RAVIOLI	37
STRAWBERRY CHOCOLATE PASTA	41
REFERENCES	45
ACKNOWLEDGEMENTS	47

Introduction

Around the world, various fruits feature as staples in our diets. There are a vast range of different fruits to select from. There are of course sweet fruits such as berries, sour fruit such as lemons, and savoury fruit such as pumpkin. Any fleshy part of a plant that is edible and supports seeds is considered to be fruit. With such a broad definition for what is considered fruit one can reflect on the huge variation of flavours that are available.

For most of us, the humble pasta is used as a staple in our diets. Its versatility opens up a world of gastronomic possibilities. Most of us would not consider mixing the two food groups however the concept of fruit pasta has been dabbled with for many years. Recipes such as 'avocado chicken' and 'mango chicken' have previously been explored and are sometimes available on menus at various eateries.

This book not only features some tasty pre-existing recipes, but also explores new scrumptious fruit pasta options. Many of the recipes featured in this book were devised in my very own kitchen. I had fun theorising and trialling each of my creations to get it just right. Firstly, I invite you to trial my fruit pasta creations along with some other traditional fruit pasta combinations. Each meal is a tasty delight just waiting for a curious palate.

Secondly, I encourage you to try out your own cooking creations. I believe that cooking doesn't need to be a chore. It can be a means of expressing yourself and your creativity! Honestly, not every meal had worked out the first time. Some just needed to be tweaked, whilst some nights the only family members eating pasta were the dogs! The fun is in trying something new and potentially unearthing a true culinary delight!

Happy cooking and bon appetit!

Jane Amparis

Creamy Avocado Chicken Fusilli
(Serves 4)

The natural creamy texture of the avocado truly enhances the rest of this smooth cream-based sauce. If you are the mood for a nice comforting meal, I recommend substituting in an egg-noodle pasta. It will really give this dish some flare!

Ingredients

500g fusilli pasta	500g chicken breast, diced
1 tbsp olive oil	2 tbsp pine nuts
600mL cooking cream	1 ripe avocado, mashed
½ cup tasty cheese, grated	Salt to taste
1 avocado sliced to garnish	

Method

1. Bring a large size saucepan of lightly salted water to a boil. Add fusilli pasta to water and boil until al dente. Strain pasta.
2. Meanwhile heat olive oil in a large heavy-based fry pan over a medium-high heat.
3. Salt chicken and add to fry pan. Stir fry chicken for two minutes.
4. Add pine nuts and continue to stir fry chicken until lightly browned.
5. Add cream and avocado. Bring to boil then simmer and reduce sauce, stirring occasionally.
6. Once sauce has reduced, add tasty cheese and mix through pasta.
7. Serve and garnish with sliced avocado.

Creamy Avocado Chicken Fusilli

💡 Tips and Tricks

- Whenever a creamy sauce is used, a thick pasta type works best as the thicker sauce needs something to cling to.

- To remove the avocado seed, chop into the seed with the heel of a knife enough so that you encounter resistance if you push any further. Then give the knife a ¼ turn and the seed should twist free.

- For an extra creamy taste, try substituting the cooking cream for thickened cream. If you do this be sure to cook over a medium heat and stir frequently to prevent cream from curdling.

Caramelised Apple with Radiatori in Tomato Sauce
(Serves 4)

The seeds for inspiration for this dish were planted when I was making Riley his baby food whilst boiling up some pasta for my own lunch. We trialled it for dinner one night and never looked back.

Ingredients

500g radiatori pasta	½ brown onion, diced	1 tbsp olive oil
150g mild pancetta, diced	700g passata	1 tbsp tomato paste
1 red apple, cored, thinly sliced	2 tsp brown sugar	2 tsp butter, melted
½ tsp cinnamon, ground	2 tbsp parsley, chopped	2 tbsp basil, chopped
Salt and pepper to taste	½ cup parmesan cheese, grated	Basil sprig to garnish

Method

1. Bring a large size saucepan of lightly salted water to a boil. Add radiatori pasta to water and boil until al dente. Strain pasta.
2. Meanwhile heat olive oil in a large heavy-based fry pan over a medium-high heat and stir fry onion until tender.
3. Add pancetta and continue to stir fry until lightly browned.
4. Add passata, tomato paste and spices. Bring to boil then simmer and reduce sauce, stirring occasionally.
5. Meanwhile core and cut the apple into thin slices.
6. Heat a medium-sized skillet over a medium-high heat to melt butter.
7. Add apple and brown sugar to butter and stir frequently for 2-3 minutes until apple is golden brown. Set apples aside. Also set aside syrup.
8. Once sauce has reduced, mix through apple, pasta and add parmesan cheese.
9. Serve and garnish with a basil sprig.

Caramelised Apple with Radiatori in Tomato Sauce

💡 Tips and Tricks

- Always taste-test the sauce before serving. Occasionally when preparing a tomato-based sauce the sauce will taste too tart. Add some of the residue syrup used from the caramelisation.

- Any red apple variety can be used when caramelising apples. Pink lady apples just work particularly well in this dish.

Hawaiian Pasta Bake
(Serves 4)

You've heard of spaghetti-pizza? Well this is a pizza-pasta. Although this dish is tasty without being put through the oven, there is something magical about the taste of caramelised pasta.

Ingredients

500g penne pasta	½ brown onion, diced
100g ham, diced	50g chorizos, diced
1 tbsp tomato paste	240g tinned pineapple, diced
2 tbsp oregano, chopped	Salt & pepper to taste
1 tbsp olive oil	700g passata
100g mozzarella cheese, chopped	

Method

1. Preheat oven to 180°C (or 160°C for fan-forced oven).
2. Bring a large size saucepan of lightly salted water to a boil. Add penne pasta to water and boil until al dente. Strain pasta.
3. Meanwhile heat olive oil in a large heavy-based fry pan over a medium-high heat and stir fry onion until tender.
4. Add ham and chorizos. Stir fry for 2 minutes.
5. Add passata, tomato paste, pineapple and herbs/spices. Bring to boil then leave to simmer, stirring occasionally.
6. Once sauce is reduced, mix through pasta.
7. Transfer to a deep-sided baking tray. Sprinkle cheese over pasta.
8. Put into oven and bake for 20mins.
9. Slice to serve.

 *Tips and Tricks*

A 800g tinned crushed Italian style tomatoes can be used as a substitute for passata

Vermicelli With Bread Crumbs, Tuna, Parsley and Lemon
(Serves 4)

I am simply addicted to this pasta dish. I frequently whip it up for lunch if I want to eat something with a little more substance than a sandwich.

Ingredients

500g vermicelli pasta	2 tbsp butter, melted
175g sourdough bread, chopped into course breadcrumbs	125g (1⅓ cups) parmesan cheese, grated
350g canned tuna, drained	⅔ cup continental parsley, chopped
Chopped zest and juice of 1 lemon	2 Cloves garlic, crushed
Salt & pepper to taste	Continental parsley sprig to garnish

Method

1. Bring a large size saucepan of lightly salted water to a boil. Add vermicelli pasta to water and boil until al dente. Strain pasta.
2. Meanwhile heat butter in a large heavy-based fry pan over a medium heat and stir fry breadcrumbs for 4-5mins. Stir frequently until breadcrumbs are golden and crunchy.
3. Increase heat to a medium-high heat.
4. Add garlic, parsley, lemon zest, juice, tuna, salt and pepper. Cook briefly.
5. Toss pasta through sauce and coat well with tuna mix.
6. Mix through grated parmesan.
7. Serve and garnish with a sprig of continental parsley.

Vermicelli With Bread Crumbs, Tuna, Parsley and Lemon

💡 Tips and Tricks

- *Vermicelli is a long, delicate strand of pasta. It is thicker than angel hair, but still benefits from being served in a light sauce.*

- *Any long, thin pasta shape can be suitably substituted for vermicelli if it is not available.*

Creamy Mango Chicken Rigatoni
(Serves 4)

When I first saw this sauce combination listed on a menu at a family restaurant it had challenged my preconceptions of what a pasta sauce should be. However, upon trying it I found this sauce to be surprisingly tasty. It has a delightfully unique flavour that has you wanting more.

Ingredients

500g rigatoni pasta	500g chicken breast, diced
1 tbsp olive oil	½ brown onion, diced
½ green capsicum, thinly sliced	3 cloves garlic, minced
1 mango, peeled, deseeded and chopped	600mL thickened cream
Salt & pepper to taste	Parsley sprig to garnish

Method

1. Bring a large size saucepan of lightly salted water to a boil. Add rigatoni pasta to water and boil until al dente. Strain pasta.
2. Meanwhile heat ½ the olive oil in a large heavy-based fry pan over a medium heat.
3. Salt chicken and add to fry pan. Cook chicken for 10 minutes or until juices run clear. Remove from heat and set aside.
4. Heat the remaining oil in the heavy-based fry pan, and cook the onion and capsicum until tender.
5. Add the garlic, ginger and mango and cook for 5 mins, or until the mango is soft.
6. Gradually add in the cream and cook for 5 minutes until sauce has reduced.
7. Return the chicken to the heavy-based fry pan and add pasta, salt & pepper.
8. Serve and garnish with parsley sprigs.

Creamy Mango Chicken Rigatoni

💡 Tips and Tricks

- When selecting a ripe mango look for a plump fruit that is weighty for its size. It should also be fragrant when you hold it under your nose. You should also be able to indent them slightly with your thumb.

- Alternatively, an unripened mango left at room temperature should ripen in a few days.

- To prepare the mango, slice through one side of the fruit alongside the stone and repeat for the other side. With a knife cut the peel away from the fruit stuck to the stone. With a large spoon you can then scoop out the mango flesh for cooking.

Spaghetti in Semi-Dried Tomato Butter Sauce
(Serves 4)

Now I've included this recipe because *technically* tomato and olives are fruits... but quite frankly it is too yummy to leave out! This dish is a great lunch option or whenever you just want a tasty and light meal.

Ingredients

500g spaghetti pasta	60g butter
½ brown onion, diced	4 rashers of bacon, diced
100g chorizos, sliced	175g sourdough bread, coarsely crumbed
2 tbsp basil leaves, chopped	200g semi-dried tomatoes
Salt to taste	Basil sprigs to garnish

Method

1. Bring a large size saucepan of lightly salted water to a boil. Add spaghetti to water and boil until al dente. Strain pasta.
2. Meanwhile heat butter in a large heavy-based fry pan over a medium-high heat and stir fry onions until tender.
3. Add bacon, chorizos and breadcrumbs. Stir fry for 2 minutes or until chorizos have caramelised.
4. Add basil, semi-dried tomatoes and olives. Stir fry further for 1 minute.
5. Toss pasta through sauce and coat well.
6. Garnish with basil sprig.

 **Tips and Tricks**

In the absence of sourdough bread, I sometimes toast a slice of multigrain bread and use that for breadcrumbs instead.

Orange, Cranberry, Walnut & Turkey Farfalle
(Serves 4)

This Christmas inspired recipe is a hit all year around! It is great for Christmas turkey leftovers or can be made economically with turkey drumsticks throughout the year.

Ingredients

500g farfalle pasta	500g turkey, roasted
½ tbsp olive oil	½ brown onion, diced
2 tbsp parsley leaves, chopped	¼ cup dried cranberries (craisins)
1 cup roasted walnuts, chopped	Juice of 2 oranges
60g butter	2 cloves garlic, crushed
Salt & pepper to taste	4 slices of multigrain bread, toasted and chopped into coarse breadcrumbs
2 tbsp extra butter for frying	

Method

1. Bring a large size saucepan of lightly salted water to a boil. Add farfalle pasta to water and boil until al dente. Strain pasta.
2. Meanwhile heat olive oil in a large heavy-based fry pan over a medium-high heat and stir fry onions until tender.
3. Lightly salt turkey and add to fry pan. Stir occasionally until turkey has lightly browned.
4. Add butter, garlic, walnuts, craisins, parsley and seasoning. Stir fry 2 minutes.
5. Add orange juice and pasta. Cook until moisture has absorbed. Set aside.
6. Meanwhile in medium sized skillet, melt butter over medium heat.
7. Add breadcrumbs to skillet and stir fry for 4-5mins until golden brown.
8. Stir through golden breadcrumbs and serve.

 **Tips and Tricks**

For a stronger orange flavour, mix the pulp of the orange juice through your pasta sauce.

Roast Pumpkin, Pancetta & Sweet Onions Gnocchi

(Serves 4)

Well here I go being cheeky by including pumpkin. This savoury flavoured fruit is often misconceived as a humble veg. This flavoursome chunky-style sauce makes it ideal for a solid pasta shape such as gnocchi.

Ingredients

1Kg gnocchi pasta	400g pumpkin, diced
Olive Oil (for drizzling)	Salt & pepper to taste
½ tbsp olive oil	1 sweet onions, diced
2 tbso thyme leaves, chopped	300g pancetta, diced
½ cup parmesan cheese, grated	2 cloves garlic, crushed

Method

1. Preheat oven to 180°C (or 160°C for fan-forced oven).
2. Place the pumpkin on a baking tray and drizzle with olive oil and season with salt, pepper and sugar.
3. Roast in oven for 30 mins.
4. Meanwhile heat 2 tbsp olive oil in a large heavy-based fry pan over a low heat and stir fry onions, thyme, salt and pepper for 20-30 mins. Cook until onions are tender and slightly coloured.
5. Bring a large size saucepan of lightly salted water to a boil. Add gnocchi pasta to water and boil until gnocchi rise to the surface. Cook for a further 3 minutes. Strain pasta.
6. Turn up heat of sauce to medium-high and add pancetta. Cook for 3-4 minutes until pancetta is crispy.
7. Add pumpkin, parsley and grated parmesan.
8. Toss pasta through chunky sauce and coat well, then serve.

 **Tips and Tricks**

Sweet onion provides a milder onion flavouring compared to brown onions. Use shallots if sweet onions are not available.

Duck L'Orange Curly Tagliatelle
(Serves 4)

This recipe is an interesting take on a traditional duck meal that has been specially adapted to a pasta dish. Be prepared for the sweet flavours of the honey, oranges to be delightfully complimented by a mild tang from the vinegar.

Ingredients

500g curly tagliatelle pasta	4 chicken stock cubes	½ tbsp olive oil
2 shallots, diced	500g duck breast, diced	4 baby carrots, julienne
Orange rind twist to garnish	Juice from 3 oranges	2 tbsp white vinegar
2 tbsp butter	2 celery stalk, julienne	2 tbsp thyme leaves, chopped
Salt and pepper to taste	2 tbsp honey	

Method

1. Bring a large size saucepan water to a boil. Add chicken stock cubes and stir through until dissolved.
2. Add tagliatelle pasta to water and boil until al dente. Strain pasta.
3. Meanwhile heat olive oil in a large heavy-based fry pan over a medium heat and stir fry shallots until tender.
4. Add duck and season with salt and pepper. Stir fry until meat has lightly browned.
5. Add carrots and celery. Stir fry for 3-4 minutes.
6. Add orange juice, vinegar, butter, honey and thyme. Simmer sauce.
7. Once sauce is reduced, mix through pasta.
8. Serve and garnish with orange rind twist.

Duck L'Orange Curly Tagliatelle

💡 Tips and Tricks

- This is a delicious way of using any left-over duck if you had prepared 'Duck Confit' earlier in the week.
- Shallots have a milder onion flavour than a brown onion and are highly recommended for this meal.

Red Grape & Chicken Rollini
(Serves 4)

The combination of grapes and chicken were originally used in my cooking when I was making Riley's baby food. Happily, it's evolution to a pasta sauce proved to be very delicious.

Ingredients

500g rollini pasta	500g chicken breast, diced
½ brown onion, diced	700g passata
200g red seedless grapes, crushed	1 ½ tbsp red wine
2 tbsp parsley, chopped	½ cup parmesan cheese, grated
Salt and pepper to taste	½ tbsp olive oil
2 tbsp tomato paste	2 tbsp sage, chopped

Method

1. Bring a large size saucepan of lightly salted water to a boil. Add rollini pasta to water and boil until al dente. Strain pasta.
2. Meanwhile heat olive oil in a large heavy-based fry pan over a medium-high heat stir fry onions until tender.
3. Salt chicken and add to fry pan. Stir-fry until lightly browned.
4. Add passata, tomato paste, red wine, grapes and spices. Bring to boil then simmer and reduce sauce, stirring occasionally.
5. Once sauce is reduced, toss pasta through chunky sauce and add parmesan. Stir through and coat pasta.
6. Garnish with parsley sprig.

 **Tips and Tricks**

Always taste-test the sauce before serving. Occasionally when preparing a tomato-based sauce the sauce will taste too tart. A splash of milk will help neutralise the acidity and take this tartness away.

Lime Lamb with Spinach Fettuccine
(Serves 4)

The lime adds a pleasant bite and its flavour infuses itself thoroughly throughout this dish.

Ingredients

500g spinach fettuccine	500g lamb, diced
½ tbsp olive oil	Juice from 2 limes
2 tbsb coriander leaves, chopped	¼ tsp ground paprika
Salt & pepper to taste	Knob of butter to garnish

Method

1. Bring a large size saucepan of lightly salted water to a boil. Add spinach fettuccine pasta to water and boil until al dente. Strain pasta.
2. Meanwhile heat olive oil in a large heavy-based fry pan over a medium-high heat and add lamb.
3. Season lamb with salt and pepper, then stir fry until meat has browned.
4. Add and stir through cooked pasta, coriander, paprika and lime juice. Cook briefly.
5. Serve and garnish with a knob of butter.

Tips and Tricks

As the lime juice infuses its flavour so readily, a thick pasta shape can be utilised without running the risk of losing the sauce flavour amongst the noodles.

Blueberry Ricotta Cannelloni
(Serves 8)

For something a bit different, try this dessert pasta at your next dinner party.

Ingredients — General

16 cannelloni shells	Non-stick cooking spray	Extra fresh blueberries to garnish

Ingredients — Filling

500g ricotta cheese	¼ cup caster sugar	¼ cup thickened cream
1 large egg	1 cup fresh blueberries	¾ cup dried cranberries (craisins)
½ tsp almond extract		

Ingredients — Topping

75 g butter, soft	¼ cup self-raising flower	½ cup brown sugar
1 tsp lemon zest, finely grated	½ cup sliced almonds	½ cup rolled oats

Method — Filling

1. Start by beating ricotta, caster sugar and cream with an electric mixer in a large-sized bowl. Beat until smooth.
2. Add egg and beat again until smooth.
3. Add blueberries, craisins and almond extract and mix through thoroughly.
4. Cover the bowl with plastic wrap and refrigerate filling until ready to use.

Method — Topping

1. Make topping in a medium size bowl. Start by crumbling butter, sugar and flour together with your fingers.
2. Add lemon zest, almonds and rolled oats and continue to crumble until loosely combine.

Blueberry Ricotta Cannelloni

Method

1. Preheat oven to 180°C (or 160°C for fan-forced oven).
2. Bring a large size saucepan of lightly salted water to a boil. Add cannelloni and parboil them for 5 mins.
3. Strain cannelloni and run under cold water. Then set them aside on a lint-free tea towel, ensuring that the shells do not touch.
4. Prepare a deep-sided baking tray by spraying with non-stick cooking oil and set aside.
5. Spoon filling into shells.
6. Place shells into baking tray and sprinkle topping over cannelloni.
7. Cover baking tray with aluminium foil and bake for 30 minutes.
8. Remove foil and bake for another 10 minutes.
9. Remove from oven and allow to stand for 10 minutes before serving.
10. Garnish with fresh blueberries.

💡 Tips and Tricks

- *If cannelloni is unavailable, use precooked lasagne sheets. Simply place the filling in a row and roll lasagne sheet over itself to create the cannelloni shape.*

- *Depending on the size, 1 lasagne sheet should substitute for 1-2 cannelloni shell(s).*

- *Alternatively, fill large-sized, precooked conchiglie (shell-shape) pasta as a substitute for cannelloni.*

Chocolate Raspberry Ravioli
(Serves 4)

The chocolate raspberry ravioli makes for a decadent dessert. Other fruit jams can work just as well.

Ingredients

200g dark chocolate, broken into pieces	2 cups plain flower	Mint leaves to garnish
2 tbsp olive oil	2 tbsp water	Extra flour (as needed)
Bowl of water (as needed)	1 egg extra	2 tbsp cold water
Raspberries to garnish	2 eggs	Whipped cream to garnish
Shaved chocolate to garnish		1 cup raspberry jam for filling

Method for Pasta Dough

1. Place plain flour, eggs and olive oil into a large mixing bowl. Set aside.
2. Put dark chocolate into a large heatproof bowl.
3. Melt chocolate over a low heat by placing heatproof bowl over a saucepan half-filled with water. Take care not allow any water to touch the bowl nor allow any water to touch the chocolate. DO NOT melt chocolate over a direct heat.
4. Stir chocolate frequently until it has completely melted, then remove from heat.
5. Add melted chocolate and stir through thoroughly then knead dough.
6. Gradually add water, 1 tsp at a time until dough is has smooth consistency to touch.
7. Knead dough on a cool surface
8. If the dough is too sticky and adheres itself to your fingers excessively, transfer the dough onto a lightly floured surface and continue to knead until dough has reached a smooth consistency. However, if the dough feels grainy and/or rough, dip your hands in water to add a small amount of moisture, and then continue to knead until dough has smooth consistency.
9. Wrap the pasta dough in cling-wrap and refrigerate for at least an hour.
10. Make an egg wash by adding the additional egg and water together and lightly whisk. Set aside.
11. Take the pasta dough out of fridge and let it rest for 15mins.
12. Work dough again until softened and then use a rolling pin to flatten.

Chocolate Raspberry Ravioli

Method for Filling

1. Lay a flattened dough sheet over a ravioli tray, and shape indents for filling. You may need to run a knife blade underneath the rolled pasta dough before you are able to freely transfer it onto the ravioli tray.
2. Lightly press on the base sheet to create wells and spoon filling into each well.
3. Using a pastry brush, egg wash the ravioli edges.
4. Lay another dough sheet on top. With a rolling pin, roll the dough onto the ravioli tray to seal the ravioli. Take care to squeeze out all the air from the ravioli pouches before sealing the pasta.
5. Cut the ravioli into their individual pieces.
6. Meanwhile, bring a large size saucepan of water to a boil. Add ravioli pasta to water and stir occasionally with a slotted spoon.
7. Boil until ravioli rise to the surface. Cook for a further 3 minutes. Strain pasta.
8. Garnish with raspberries, mint leaves and shaved chocolate.

Tips and Tricks

- If you do not own a ravioli tray or ravioli attachment for a pasta machine, try using a round 7cm diameter cookie cutter to form each piece. Seal the ravioli by pressing the edges of the dough together with a fork.

- Alternatively, use a cookie cutter with a larger diameter and encase the filling by folding the pasta in half to make agnolotti. Seal pasta pouch using fork.

- Do not overfill ravioli. Only place ½ tsp of filling per ravioli.

- Always ensure that all the air has been squeezed out of the ravioli pouches before sealing as trapped air will expand during the cooking process and destroy your ravioli.

Strawberry Chocolate Pasta
(Serves 4)

Warning! This dessert is very moreish. There is nothing like the complimentary flavour of strawberries and chocolate, but this one has a delightful twist.

Ingredients

1 batch Chocolate Pasta (see Chocolate Raspberry Ravioli)	250g strawberries, hulled and sliced
2 tbsp butter	2 tbsp brown sugar
1/3 cup balsamic vinegar	1/2 tsp mild paprika
1 tsp rosemary leaves	Pepper to taste
Extra strawberries to garnish	

Method

1. Make chocolate pasta by following the procedure outlined in steps 1-10 of the 'chocolate raspberry ravioli' recipe.
2. Shape pasta as desired.
3. Meanwhile, bring a large size saucepan of water to a boil. Add chocolate pasta to water cook until al dente. Strain pasta.
4. Meanwhile heat a medium-sized skillet over a medium heat to melt butter.
5. Add strawberries and sugar. Sauté for 2 minutes, stirring frequently.
6. Add balsamic vinegar and seasoning. Simmer sauce, stirring occasionally.
7. Once sauce is reduced, mix through pasta
8. Serve and garnish with fresh strawberries.

Strawberry Chocolate Pasta

💡 Tips and Tricks

- ✓ As making pasta from scratch is a very time consuming process you may consider making it in advance. The pasta will keep well overnight in the fridge provided that they are covered in plastic wrap or can keep in the freezer for a month.

- ✓ Frozen pasta can be put straight into boiling water. Just bear in mind that they will take longer to cook.

References

Some of the recipes in this book have been adapted from the following sources:

AllRecipes. (Oct, 2012). *Creamy Chicken and Mango Pasta.* Retrieved from http://allrecipes.com.au/recipe/16944/creamy-chicken-and-mango-pasta.aspx

Campion, A. & Curtis, M. (2008). *In the Kitchen: More Than 1000 Recipes For Every Day.* Melbourne: Hardie Grant Books.

NewsLifeMedia. (Oct, 2012). *Chicken Avocado Fettuccine: Recipe #3658.* Retrieved from http://www.bestrecipes.com.au/recipe/chicken-avocado-fettuccine-L3658.html

TreStelle. (Sept, 2012). *Blueberry Ricotta Dessert Lasagna.* Retrieved from http://www.trestelle.ca/english/recipegallery/getrecipe.php?recipeid=375

Acknowledgements

Thank you to everybody that made this *Fruity Pasta Sensations* possible.

Thank you to Pauline Langmead from *PL Inc* for all her efforts she has placed into taking the stunning photos for this book. Pauline, you make the meals look so tasty, I want to eat food right off the pages!

A huge thank you to Amy Buglass, Maria Gurgius, Mina Gurgius, Kirsty Hayes, Lori Bulmer, Heidi McDowell, Dollie Amparis, Roger Amparis and George-Eric Amparis for all the 'behind the scenes' help you have given me. Without your valuable contributions and your time this project could never have operated so smoothly and successfully.

Finally, a big thank you to my husband, Jean-Paul for his part in supporting this project every step of the way. I appreciate the way you had never hesitated when I approached with the bold idea of getting *Fruity Pasta Sensations* published. I also value your input and honest feedback during the development stages of my recipes. All of these recipes are better for it. Thank you for believing in me.

www.ingramcontent.com/pod-product-compliance
Lightning Source LLC
Chambersburg PA
CBHW042052290426
44110CB00001B/34